AF426946

...AND GOD SPOKE

...AND GOD SPOKE

A STORY OF SHAME TO GLORY

JULIE HOLDER

...And God Spoke
A Story of Shame to Glory
© 2024 by Julie Holder

All rights reserved solely by the author. The author guarantees all contents are original and do not infringe upon the legal rights of any other person or work. No part of this book may be reproduced in any form without the permission of the author.

Scriptures marked KJV are taken from the KING JAMES VERSION (KJV): KING JAMES
VERSION, public domain.
Scriptures marked NIV are taken from the NEW INTERNATIONAL VERSION (NIV):
Scripture taken from THE HOLY BIBLE, NEW INTERNATIONAL VERSION ®. Copyright©
1973, 1978, 1984, 2011 by Biblica, Inc.™. Used by permission of Zondervan
Scriptures marked ESV are taken from the THE HOLY BIBLE, ENGLISH STANDARD
VERSION (ESV): Scriptures taken from THE HOLY BIBLE, ENGLISH STANDARD
VERSION ® Copyright© 2001 by Crossway, a publishing ministry of Good News Publishers.
Used by permission.

Printed in the United States of America.
ISBN-13: 979-8-218-54062-3
Library of Congress Control Number: 2024922826

JDH Press
Lenox, Michigan

CONTENTS

PREFACE

H i, and oh my! I have to say, I never thought I would write a book. I never thought I would be sharing some of the most intimate experiences of my life with the world. I never thought I would write a "testimony" song… and then, God spoke.

Let me start by introducing myself. My name is Julie Dee Holder, Child of God. Daughter of the King. I am now 54 years young and still a spunky soul; just now, an obedient soul in the name of Jesus! Obedience has not always been my forte — just ask my parents! Like many who have grown up in a loving Christian household, I grew up knowing Jesus and expectations: the ten commandments and all the important stuff. I was blessed to be born into a family who made sure I knew God as my heavenly father; that His son died on the cross for my sins and yours too! I learned to acknowledge that Jesus was, and still is, the ultimate sacrifice. What a beautiful gift that has been in my life! However, as I emerged into the teenage years, life began to prove as a test;

offering up much temptation, misdirection, lies, and sin. Fulfilling all *my* earthly desires.

In telling the truths behind my testimony, I truly pray that you will be able to relate. My prayer is for this story to bless you, if even just one person, into completing or perhaps beginning your own circle of God's obedience. Inviting Him to bless you abundantly as the father encourages you to step into your own calling!

CHAPTER 1

P roviding you with some history of my trials may prove to offer a better understanding of how I ended up *here*, the best place I could be: in the presence of my Father, Son and the Holy Spirit. A place of complete peace, joy and thankfulness. So here it is. Thank you for joining me on this journey and for reading my story!

Unfortunately, as a teenager sin and temptation crept in. I fell victim to my own flesh; a victim to the lies of the devil and the insecurities that his minions spewed upon me. I grew up a bit "thick" or "fluffy", if you will. I never felt pretty enough, skinny enough (or at all for that matter), and not as smart. I felt I was never good enough in general, which led me to seek the acceptance and approval of others, especially the boys, then the guys, then the men. This was not good… not good at all. I felt that if I had a boyfriend, even at a young age, then I was "good enough" for someone, even if it was the wrong one. I equated having a boyfriend as a source of happiness and feeling complete.

I had my first boyfriend at the age of 14. Of course, I was still a virgin at that time. Unfortunately, that gift of being pure was swiftly stolen from me. I had been dating a boy for six months or so, hanging out at the mall and going to movies; just doing the things "kids" do, right? One Superbowl Sunday, all the adults were going to be at a party next door at the neighbors', so my parents let us kids have our own Superbowl party, and I invited this boyfriend over. I was so excited! As it would turn out, this less-than-fine fella ended up stealing my innocence. He raped me in my own room, with all the other kids down in the noise filled basement. The boy who I thought liked me; the boy that I thought I could trust.

Prior to that exact moment, I never dreamed that I was in harm's way. I was naive and trusted him. Regardless of your age, you always put yourself at a risk of danger when you enter the dating pool. For instance, back then, we did not have internet dating or social media. How well do you truly know someone that you may have met online? I thought I knew this boy, as we had been hanging out in person, for months! As it turned out, I didn't. The bottom line is, I never should have put myself in such a situation where he had the opportunity to take advantage of me. It never crossed my mind not to isolate myself with him, with no one else around to help me or hear my cries for help.

This experience turned my expectations of what sex and intimacy should be into something shameful and jaded. Looking back, I see that this action could have influenced me, and shaped me in a multitude of different directions. Luckily, it made me a bit scared of sex and mistrusting of men. I didn't want another experience like that traumatic event. I was never a promiscuous teenager, but in my mind, I felt that sex would be expected and necessary to keep the boyfriends I would encounter as I matured. I started losing sight of God's will and expectations of me and for me. I started serving sin out of insecurity and from an inability to fight my own fleshly desires. The adversary had planted destructive lies in my head, using my own mind as his warring battlefield. He led me to believe that if I did not do certain things asked of me, the male counterpart would leave me for someone who would; I believed that it was required or considered a part of my womanly duties to please him, and that if it felt good, it was good. If he said he "loved" me, then it was acceptable. Oh, how easy words can deceive one's heart swaying them towards a path of heartbreak, sorrow and destruction.

REFLECT

CHAPTER 2

At the time of adolescence, many of my friends had sex with just about anyone who showed them attention. Perhaps it was out of insecurity, neediness or a wanting to feel desirable or loved. Some of them just used sex to manipulate the fellas into doing what they needed or wanted them to do. Others had kids at very young ages and forfeited their childhood for parenthood. I wasn't any of those girls. I never was one, and certainly did not approve of those behaviors—as if my actions and my sins were better than theirs? More lies from the devil, who was just prowling around like a lion, waiting to seek, steal and destroy whomever he could, including me. Somewhere in the back of my brain, along with the conviction of the holy spirit in the depths of my gut, I knew not to just sleep around for the fun of it or to use my body as a manipulation tool. I would wait until I fell in love, gave my heart to "the" guy, *and then* would give him my body. In my young brain, and even as I matured, I felt like, "hey, this makes sense, right?" My thought process was that in doing that, my sin was far less.

Years later, I learned that is *not* how that works! I was trying to validate my own sin and make myself believe that Jesus would judge me differently—just me, independently. He judges us by our hearts, doesn't He? So clearly, He knew I wasn't loose or promiscuous! I did not lay down for *just anyone*. I only laid down with whomever had my heart... at that time. Sadly enough, I was fooling myself, but I was not fooling my Heavenly Father, the one who sees and hears all. Jesus does judge us by our hearts, but it is so much more than that. He desires for us to be different, to stand out from the masses, to shine our light in representation of "Him", our Heavenly Father.

Hebrews 13:4 considers sex outside of marriage to be immoral:

> "Let marriage be held in honor among all and let the marriage bed be undefiled for God will judge the sexually immoral and adulterous." (ESV)

Jeremiah 17:10 states:

> "I the lord search the heart and examine the mind, to reward each person according to their conduct, according to what their deeds deserve." (NIV)

Romans 12:2 exhorts us saying:

> "And be not conformed to this world, but be ye transformed by the renewing of your mind, that ye may prove what is good, and acceptable, and of the perfect will of God." (KJV)

1 Samuel 16:7 declares:

> "So, God judges you by what is in your heart, by your earnest efforts; rather than by what you can accomplish through your actions".

One of the greatest compliments that anyone can give you is to say that you are *different*! Meaning they see the Jesus in you!

REFLECT

CHAPTER 3

I was married young and lived with my first husband for a few years before we married. I mean, everyone tries on the jeans before you buy them, don't they? Honestly, I knew he wasn't the best choice to take as a husband, but I loved him. I really did. And of course, he made me feel special, "acceptable", and loved. I had no idea what love even meant; at least not the healthy love I should have had for myself, being the daughter of the King, and surely not the "love" a husband was supposed to show his wife. The same love that Jesus had for His church, His bride.

My husband was broken and did not know love himself. The marriage was a mess, doomed from the very beginning, and eventually ended in divorce when I was 30 years old. I prayed intently and desperately for two years asking God to either repair and restore the marriage, or to remove me. After his cheating, stealing, lying, abusing drugs and a failed attempt at rehabilitation, I was released and became the owner of a brand-new divorce. There was a feeling of epic failure in one of the most important commitments (not to mention covenants of God) that people make in a lifetime, creating more insecurities and giving the devil more room to spew his deceitful untruths in my direction.

Here is where we really start cutting into the "meat" of this dish. After a long recovery and healing period, I finally decided to enter the dating world again. Wow. Just flippin' wow, okay? Thirty-one and single. The dating pool left much to be desired—and I mean much. Did I say "wow" already? Still riddled with insecurity, doubt, shame, fear, and now loneliness, the enemy had a lot to work with. The adversary saw fresh blood and he licked his chops, seeing my brokenness and vulnerability. He dove right in with delight. It was sad, but I was kind of clueless; and again, just wanted to love and be loved. At least I had some idea of my own self-worth and knew better as to what *I did not want* in my next relationship.

The most disappointing aspect of the ordeal was that I had no idea that my own self-love and the love of Jesus could have, and should have, been enough! To let Him lead, and let God provide the right man at the right time, when I might actually be ready to receive such a person. In reflecting back to that time, I ask these questions: did I let the Father speak into me? To lead me? Did I allow myself to soak in *His* wisdom, love, obedience and faithfully seek *His* guidance as I began this new chapter in my life? No, I absolutely did not. I carnally moved forward, very much believing that I had total control of my life's decisions. Big mistake...Big mistake!

REFLECT

CHAPTER 4

Needless to say, I journeyed into the dating process. It was crazy. I dated several fellas, most only once or twice because the red flags were so apparent. However, I never slept with any of them; that is, until I entered a committed relationship and until I knew I was completely in love with that person. Again, not wanting to admit that I was validating my own sin saying, "God judges us by our hearts. He knows me!" My poor mom would warn me time and again when the opportunity arose in conversation. She would say, "you know you should not be having sex out of marriage!" My response? With fingers in my ears, "la la la I can't hear you!" Or, I would give her the excuse of how the Lord knows my heart and would judge me accordingly. I would feel the Holy Spirit convict me, but clearly, I was not strong enough and not willing enough to fight my own flesh. I would ignore my convictions and continue doing life my way, not seeking God's direction. I wasn't asking God what He wanted or what He thought, because ultimately, I knew what my Father thought, and what He wanted, but I wasn't willing to respond; to be obedient and ultimately become totally dependent on my Heavenly Father. The One who created me, knew me best, and loved me most.

After a couple of long-term relationships and 15 years later, I met another man. I innocently stopped for a wash and blowout for my crazy hair and met a sweet young lady. By the end of the appointment, she said she wanted to introduce me to her single dad. I told her I was on a break and not accepting applications, but she basically sold him to me in that moment. It was so precious: a daughter trying to find her father a good mate. Two years later, we were married; five years following that, we were divorced. This story, unfortunately, is a whole different book in and of itself. Once again, I married someone who, himself, was broken and carried many heavy, generational chains. I was told I was the third marriage, but really, I was the fifth. I was told he had three children, which soon turned into four. After five long years of marriage, one emotional breakdown, and six months of therapy, he was diagnosed as a manipulative narcissist.

Ultimately, after five long years of crying every day and begging Jesus to fix this marriage or release me (sound familiar?), God so *mercifully* removed me from this unhealthy relationship. However, the true blessing that came of this experience, is that I have been blessed with an absolutely beautiful, smart, loving and kind daughter! She was almost 11-years-old when I met her, and now she will soon be turning 22. Her mother had previously graduated to Heaven and I am beyond honored that she and Jesus chose me to represent and be there to love her precious child, who needed a mother figure. My heart was given something I thought I would never experience: a daughter. Once again, God blessed me immensely. Glory be to the Father for her and the bond that continues to keep our relationship close.

REFLECT

CHAPTER 5

Moving forward, I have exited this marriage, while entering covid in parallel. It was intensely sad and painfully lonely. I had left a husband and a family and had just lost my best brother-friend of 26 years very suddenly to a heart attack. All of me was absolutely shattered; I was heartbroken to say the least. It was grueling to be isolated in my new, unfamiliar home, trying to find creative ways to bide my time. Opening yet another opportunity for the enemy to creep his way into my life using the art of distraction. I'm sure you have heard about all of the enticing social media platforms out there, including Facebook, yes? Oh boy! Well, guess what? Me too. Being alone, broken, and bored, I spent a lot of time there, and like many of us, I squandered *way too much time* scrolling through the plethora of information and memes at my disposal.

What I now realize, is that although I was experiencing much more dependence on Jesus, and had a refreshed, exciting love affair with my savior,

He deserved more of my attention. I should have been reading my Bible, worshipping and praising His name, and spending my time productively, getting to know my Father on a more personal level. I still hadn't discovered my true purpose of stepping into my calling and was not being as obedient as I should have been. However, let me say this: while I was busy setting Facebook on fire, I can happily say that I did meet some really great people, especially one in particular who captured my attention.

I met a fella that had sent me a request. We had several friends in common, so I obliged! We immediately became fast friends, which I really, truly enjoyed. I was not looking for a relationship in any way at that time, but I found he filled my time, my loneliness, and eventually my heart. He had become like a new brother-friend that I still missed so deeply. I was so happy! He also lived in another state, so how harmful could it be? Clearly, this would never turn into anything of a romantic nature, especially with several states separating us. The situation was perfect! Well, I have learned why the saying, "never say never" came into existence. So, there's that.

A few months after we became friends, I happened to be heading into his turf to visit a girl-friend of mine who also lives there. He saw that I was going to be close to his area and asked if he could come to meet me in person. I can't lie,

I found myself excited and very happily obliged. Now the story takes a whole different turn. Are you starting to see a pattern yet? Oh, the tangled webs we weave when we try to control our own lives and do not ask God to lead. One would think I had learned my lesson by now. You would assume I would recognize the red flags for what they are (even from afar), but apparently, I am a bit colorblind and chose to see them as green. I know, I am sitting here shaking my head too! Once again, I naively believed every word spoken. I truly felt that this man was genuine, authentic, and that we were developing a great, meaningful friendship and relationship. I *knew* that he cared about me and my feelings, and I knew he wanted the best for me. I soon recognized that he wanted more than a friendship with me. I eagerly absorbed his fascinating stories, trusted him and was beginning to catch intense feelings. I cannot lie, that fluttering heart felt really good! It didn't hurt that I found him incredibly attractive! I found myself captivated by his charm, kind heart, and tenderness.

On our first visit, things went so great! We were super comfortable and got along great; it was as though we had known each other for years. We had absolutely undeniable chemistry. The trouble was just brewing full speed ahead! We had so much fun! Now, please keep in mind, I wasn't then in the same place that I am now in my relationship with God. Of course, I knew Him well, but I was not walking in obedience as I should have been, putting "Him" first!

We went out to dinner with my girlfriend and her husband and then returned back to their house for drinks. It was obvious that night that my then-fling *really* liked to drink. Though, I was willing to blame it on nerves, first time meeting, blah blah, blah. We were all drinking that night! My girlfriend mentioned this observation and warned me. I took a note to self and stowed it away in the back of my brain's storage. As it goes, I am a fantastic enabler and always have been. To be honest, I'm not a big drinker—never have been. I always dabbled more in herbal refreshments, if you get my drift. I didn't think his drinking would turn into a "problem" of sorts. I figured it wouldn't affect my life, until it did.

Our friendship progressed to a whole new level after that visit. He proclaimed his feelings for me and my heart was overjoyed and that was it. Game on! Many miles separated us, so we traveled back and forth from state to state, getting to know each other the best we could in such short intervals. Nothing intimate happened at that time, but we definitely had an amazing affair of the heart! We engaged in FaceTime dates, phone chats, Facebook messages exchanging cute posts and memes... We were in constant contact. What I failed to realize was that the time I spent with my Jesus was becoming less and less. My guy and I successfully survived this long-distance love for over two years. He had absolutely captured my heart and I did indeed love him. Flaws and all I loved him, and he loved me, flaws and all. I loved him. I loved his entire family, his friends, his dogs. I loved where he lived and mostly, how he made me feel. I was all in, with my head in the clouds. Until, the summer of 2022, when he came to stay with me for ten weeks. This was the longest stint we had been together throughout our growing relationship. I figured this would be the tell-tale if we were meant to be and if we could be successful living together fulltime.

Sadly, this was when I learned how bad his drinking and partying lifestyle actually was. Without a doubt, his drinking was a problem, and it was affecting my life, my job, and how I felt about him and our potential future. His drinking problem (amongst other addictions), and the attached actions, were something that I did not want to live with. Nor did I want to help usher in his death by alcohol. I loved him too deeply for that and loved myself enough that I did not wish to experience that torment. I had been through way too much agony from death and did not want to intentionally invite more. I found myself also engaging in sinful behaviors more and more: trust me, I was not perfect either. I was right next to him ordering drinks, but not getting drunk, and smoking pot. (I mean God made grass and it was natural right?) I was also behaving in a way that was unclean; engaging in sex without being married did not allow me to portray the proper picture of a Christian woman. Now is when the gut-wrenching struggle of spiritual awakening begins.

REFLECT

CHAPTER 6

Fortunately for me, despite all that was going on, I continued growing closer to the Father and trying to win my guy over to Christ. I was leaning on my savior for help, and I thought I might have a chance of winning my love's soul for the kingdom of Jesus! I so badly wanted my guy to fall in love with Jesus and tried to sway him from his destructive lifestyle and alleviate any doubts he had about who the Holy Trinity is. I *so* badly wanted my guy to love me and Jesus *more* than sin and addiction. By the way, did I mention that my guy was unequally yoked and was basically an unbeliever? Yeah, this is probably an important fact you need to know—a fantastic recipe for destruction. Disappointingly, that last, long stay in Michigan was the beginning of the end for us. The spirit of addiction was revealing itself in his actions and his words, creating disrespect and selfishness that I could not tolerate. It also quickly became evident to my family, my friends and his friends as well. God started working and speaking loudly into me, making sure I heard *His* words and warnings. At first, I was trying to ignore them, but thankfully, God is persistent! My Creator, my Father made it quite clear that I had a choice to make; him and sin, or God and obedience. This ultimately decided my fate, because that, my friends, was a no-brainer in my book. I chose my Abba, my Jehovah, my Creator. The One who will truly always love me and never mislead me.

Jeremiah 29:11:

"For I know the plans I have for you" declares the lord, "plans to prosper you and not to harm you, plans to give you a hope and a future." (NIV)

REFLECT

CHAPTER 7

This is where the story gets really good; painfully hard, but honestly, inspirationally *good*. My guy has an amazing sister, who is married to a pastor. What are the odds that my guys' brother-in-law pastors a church in Michigan? Imagine that! God works in amazing ways! I had met them a few times and absolutely loved them! When my guy was in town, we would attend my church, not theirs, but we did meet up with them for visits and meals. Right before my guy was headed out of town, we met with his sister and husband for a luncheon. This is where my story gets real—crazy in the name of Jesus. At this particular meal, I sat across from the brother-in-law. As we were enjoying this low-key family meal, God decided to speak, again ... using him as the vessel. He looked directly into my eyes, leaned forward, and spoke words that would forever change my life's direction. Words that I will be eternally grateful for. God makes no mistakes. None. He is so good and faithful!

Let's rewind first, because God had previously convicted me about sleeping with that boyfriend and not marrying him. I once again, had ignored His gentle advisement not once, but twice now. My flesh was still weak, and my carnal desires still drove my actions. I still wanted to please man and myself. So, when the day came, I knew it was no coincidence—it was God speaking. This could be my last chance to respond, my last chance to change, to die to flesh entirely, and become obedient to my Father.

So, there sat my brother-in-law directly across from me. He asked a very simple yet direct question: "So, when am I going to do your wedding?" I almost choked on my food in that very moment. My response was quite candid, and I honestly replied, "Ummm, you're not." He then asked me why, as my guy was sitting next to me. I had to very honestly and very uncomfortably answer the question. I responded, "He has a colossal drinking problem, and I cannot and will not marry that." His response in that moment took my breath away. He leaned into me from across the table, looked me right in the eyes and said these words: "Well, I know you love Jesus and are a godly woman. Do not get caught on the wrong side of the fence." In that moment I could see Jesus' face glaring at me, and I knew without a shadow of a doubt it was the Almighty Father speaking. He was using this man as the vessel to deliver this important and urgent message for the third time. I was stunned, but I clearly picked up what Jesus was laying down. In that moment, I knew what I needed to do. But let me say this; the right thing is never the easy thing. Never. I was addicted to my boyfriend, and like every other addiction, they are so hard to break. It was hard for me, and even harder to hurt him. I knew he loved me, but I also knew he loved alcohol probably more. Lifestyle change is hard and I felt he probably would not be willing to do that in the name of love.

When my guy flew home a few days later, I knew it had to be over and what had to be done. I needed to *take my body back* in the name of Jesus Christ and start walking in a manner worthy of my calling, to which I had been called (Ephesians 4:1). It was time to give my temple back to God, after all, it is His. He lives inside of me, and inside of each and every one of us! Once I the realization of my behavior within all my relationships set in, I was sickened. I was ashamed, and knew without a doubt that I had to change. The fact that every single time I had laid down with a man not in marriage, I was defiling Jesus' temple, made me literally sick and want to vomit. The realization was beyond eye opening; it was utterly heartbreaking and made me cry out in an earnest repentance that I had never undergone before.

This act of repentance for this particular sin was like nothing I had ever felt. I had to apologize to my Father and ask Him to forgive me. It was probably the most agonizing, yet humbling action I have ever experienced in this lifetime. How beautiful is our Father who offers forgiveness and new mercy?

> The lord our God is merciful and forgiving, even though we have rebelled against him. (Dan 9:9 NIV)

Now after dropping to my knees in front of the Lord, I had to somehow muster the courage to present this to my boyfriend. How in the world was I going to tell him that we could no longer have sex until we were married, and that we could not be married until he quit drinking? This was excruciating, horrifying, and a bit overwhelming. In fact, my heart still cries out as I relive that night in my mind's eye. My heart still hurts. He was so hurt, very confused, completely shocked and justifiably a bit angry. When I envision his face, riddled with consternation and dismay it makes me a bit nauseous.

I totally expected and understood his reaction wholeheartedly. I got it. We had been having sex for two years and now, all of a sudden, it's become a problem? Frankly, I was not exactly setting the best example of how a God-loving, God-fearing

Christian woman should present herself. He knew I was a follower of Jesus and went to church every Sunday. He knew how much I loved my Jesus and strived to serve Him well, yet I was still partaking in sinful acts with him. I knew I owed him not only an explanation, but an enormous apology. I felt horrible, for him and selfishly, for me too. I loved him so much, but I also love me and most importantly, I love Jesus more. I knew it had to end.

It was a painful three-hour-long FaceTime conversation. This took place on the first Wednesday of October; October 5th of 2022 to be exact. I tried to tell him it would be best to just end it and break things off right then. I knew he had needs that I could no longer meet. I also knew he could not stop drinking. We both cried, talked and cried some more. He professed his love for me and believed he could stop the drinking, or at least reel it in to a minimal level of consumption. In my heart of hearts, I knew it would take professional help for him to do this successfully. However, he truly believed that he could do it on his own and I so badly wanted to believe him. So, the ending agreement was that he had until December 28th (the date of my flight to him) to show me that he could get it together and stop the abusive drinking. We both know how this ends right? Spoiler alert: not well.

REFLECT

CHAPTER 8

The phone dates continued, but the Friday night calls were slowing down. He didn't want to call me when he was drunk. When we did speak and I could detect he was under the influence, I would call it out and he would get mad. Anger and resentment started rearing its ugly head, which lead to ugly words, which lead to the realization that this was not headed in the right direction of healing. I reiterated that if behaviors hadn't changed by the time I was supposed to board a plane, I would not be getting on that plane. And I didn't.

I so badly wanted to go and see him with every fiber of my being, but the Holy Spirit convicted me. I knew the temptation of sin would be great once I became in the presence of the man I still loved. Ever so quickly we were approaching Christmas, and I was supposed to fly out just three days later. I had given him subtle reminders and warnings all along, but he didn't take them seriously. The day after Christmas I was still warring in the battlefield of my mind. I swiftly took myself into my prayer room and laid it down before my Abba, my Father. I was on my face, releasing full-on sobs of desperation, crying out to the Lord for help, for the answers I already knew but needed Him to confirm.

I put my closed Bible on the bed, rested on my knees, urgently requesting my Father to respond. As I spoke out loud asking for instruction and praying for the man that I loved, I heard that soft audible voice in my head. The Holy Spirit said, "open the Bible", so I did just that. But it was so strange; when I opened the Bible, I felt like it wasn't the right spot and went to reshuffle and reopen the book, but my hands were frozen in place and that soft voice said, "no." I knew God had opened His living word to the exact page I needed to read. I finished my prayers through violent sobs and tears, collected myself, wiped my eyes, and went to the kitchen to peruse what the Father wanted me to read. **1 Corinthians 5:9-13**. I anxiously studied these words in a state of astonishment. How good is our Father to answer with complete truth in that very moment?

The verse read as follows:

> *"I wrote to you in my letter not to associate with sexually immoral people, not at all meaning the people of this world who are immoral, or the greedy and swindlers, or idolators. In that case, you would have to leave this world. But now I am writing to you that you must not associate with anyone who claims to be a brother or sister but is sexually immoral or greedy, an idolator or slanderer, a drunkard or swindler. Do not even eat with such people. What business is it of mine to judge those outside of the church? Are you not to judge those inside? God will just those outside. Remove the wicked man from among yourselves."*

Wow. Just wow, wow, and wow. How good is our God? Do you see which words were capitalized? Yes, I did too. It was exactly in that moment that I knew what I had to do. I went to the phone and rang him up, telling him that nothing had changed, no improvements had taken place and that I would not be getting on that plane for our yearly Christmas holiday visit. I must admit, this was one of the hardest things I have ever done in my life, but now it is something I am probably most proud of. He was incredibly angry, hurt, and despised me for months. He blamed me for a plethora of *his* emotions, yet took zero responsibility for his lack of action throughout the whole situation. He proved to me once more of his unwillingness to change. It was incredibly heartbreaking in every way, but that was when my true healing started. That was when I finally died to my flesh. That was when my complete and utter obedience had come full circle, and I *did* take my body back in the name of Christ. I realized that perhaps while I was trying to desperately to win him over in the name of Jesus, that maybe the devil was using him to try to make me stray from my loyalty to the Lord. I don't know, it is just a thought that came to me one night while pondering the whole situation. I feel that discernment is key, and one cannot always assume that everything or everyone is sent from the Lord!

REFLECT

CHAPTER 9

It took months for my heart to heal. Even still, it hurts a bit to relive this story and share my journey with the world, but I am in such a place of peace. I am fully committed and totally in love with Jesus Christ, the one who gave it all for me, and you! My life is so different; it is so much better, happier, calmer and more peaceful. I truly live in this verse:

> "...and the peace of God, which surpasses all understanding, will guard your hearts and minds through Christ Jesus." (Phil 4:7)

The great ending to this story is this, right here! Only a few short months after my choice, I went to visit the brother-in-law, the very man that Jesus used to deliver His message to me. His name is Craig. He prophesied to me that once I stepped into my calling, God would give me a song and a book. Craig did not know I was an untrained, unsuccessful singer/songwriter, but God did. I did not know that I could write a short story book, but God did. Talk about being on fire with Holy Spirit!

So, it was then that I wrote the song *Took My Body Back*, inspired from the book of Ephesians, and started creating my album called *Eyes On You*, which tells my story through music, followed by writing my testimony story. God then conveniently brought a music producer into my life through church, who worked out of a recording studio close to my home. Imagine that? God truly provides what, or whom we need when the time is right! His name is Jessie, and I will be forever thankful for him. We are now working on song number nine out of ten. Of the tracks, eight are originals that tell my story, and two are cover songs that resonate with me and my life. I hope you will check out the CD and I pray that my songs resonate with you in your life!

REFLECT

AFTERWORD

I want to thank you from the bottom of my heart for reading this story—*my story*. What started out as a story of shame, God turned into a story of glory! He can turn what looks like a path of destruction into a road of victory!

Thank you for loving Jesus Christ and acknowledging Him as your redeemer and savior. If you haven't yet and want to, **now** is the time to introduce yourself! The Father knows you and loves you and He has been lovingly waiting for you!

We never know what God has planned for us if we continue to try and control our own lives. Let go and let God and see what happens in your life! You will be abundantly blessed and amazed at all that God has in store for you!

BE BLESSED!

REFLECTIONS

When reflecting back on my life, and as you reflect on yours, let's ask ourselves some questions and put ourselves in a state of thought awareness.

1. What have we been doing with, and in our lives with the time that we have been given?

2. What do we want to do, and who do we want to become moving forward? What are our goals? How do we want to be effective in our own life, as well as to others in their lives?

3. Do we know God and do we truly live for him? Does he get our best and our firsts in everyday? Do we trust him to lead us and then choose to follow?

4. Are we willing to be obedient to gods' will and his plans for us? For we know they are good!

5. We need to recognize that where we start, is not where we finish. We will continually encounter people and experiences that will teach us and grow us. We can use these to help others!

6. Our past mistakes and decisions do not define us. This is not who we are! They are shaping us to become a better version of ourselves. To better love and serve others in a godly lifestyle.

7. When we accept Jesus as our savior, we become new creatures in Christ. We cannot speak the same, act the same, or think the same way we used to. Our goal becomes to be more like him! Jesus doesn't expect perfection, but he expects earnest effort and he desires for us to love him and love others!

8. God gives us new mercy every single day! If we make a mistake and sin, we just call it out and ask for forgiveness. We repent for that sin and God will forgive us. He tells us to change our thought process and sin no more and he will remember our sin no more!

9. God is love. He gave his only begotten son to die a torturous death for us, overcome sin and the grave, so we could live! Who else would do that?

10. Find your joy in the Lord every day! He fills us with a peace and calm in the middle of every storm. Praise his name in the good, the bad and the sad. Even in the valleys, we are to lean into him and see him good!

11. Be merciful and forgiving to others. We do not always know what a person has gone through or is going through. "Forgive us our trespasses as we forgive those who trespass against us". God forgives us, and it is required that we forgive others; for our own peace and to receive forgiveness from the father!

12. Do all things in love. Everything we do and say should come from the heart. People recognize we are children of Christ by the fruits we bear. They see this in us; we will not need to tell them. Be the light and salt and you will bear good fruits!

BE BLESSED!

SCAN CODE TO HEAR NEW
MUSIC FROM JULIE HOLDER

JULIE
HOLDER
Eyes on you

REFLECT

www.ingramcontent.com/pod-product-compliance
Lightning Source LLC
Chambersburg PA
CBHW052123150726
48002CB00006B/2477